Networking Thoughtfully

Networking Thoughtfully

The 30-minute read that could change your life

Martin Wheadon

Matador
9 Priory Business Park,
Wistow Road, Kibworth Beauchamp,
Leicestershire. LE8 0RX
Tel: 0116 279 2299
Email: books@troubador.co.uk
Web: www.troubador.co.uk/matador
Twitter: @matadorbooks

ISBN 978 1785899 256

British Library Cataloguing in Publication Data.
A catalogue record for this book is available from the British Library.

Typeset in 10pt Gill Sans by Troubador Publishing Ltd, Leicester, UK

Matador is an imprint of Troubador Publishing Ltd

To my dear wife - taken from me too soon
by cancer

Contents

1. A Note from Martin

The 30-minute read that could change your life

Networking can revolutionise your life if you allow it to and my hope is that this booklet will help you to achieve the success in networking you desire.

I have split the content into bite-sized thoughts or reflections based on books I have read, tapes I have listened to, on watching others or from what I have learned by bitter experience. The thoughts will take you from preparing for the event, having an effective meeting, right through to the follow-up and beyond. The notes were the basis of a seminar I used to run for Lloyds TSB in central London.

Children network naturally and they are the perfect role models for what we want to achieve. They will talk without fear of rejection, have an opinion and laugh a lot. They introduce people they meet to their friends and stay in contact, texting, phoning, visiting or using the whole range of social media. This booklet is not for experts such as these but for adults who need to build relationships.

Whether you read the booklet right through from start to finish or just dip into it, I hope you will find something that will make you think and that you can use.

Martin Wheadon

2. Introduction to Networking

Thought One

Networking is just a purposeful conversation between consenting adults

You cannot force people to talk to you. If they are not interested then so be it. Do not waste your time but find others who do want to converse and tell you all about themselves. You can then build a conversation, interweaving snippets of what they have told you with your own story and why it could be mutually beneficial for the conversation to continue.

The purpose depends on what you want to achieve, something you have the freedom to decide. People at networking events are there to talk to you; they may be as nervous as you are so there should be only pleasant experiences that await you. I have found that people have hidden depths, so enjoy discovering their stories.

3. Mental Preparation

Thought Two

Networking can be a way of life that will change your world for the better. It is not just used for winning new business or making new business associates. You will also benefit by bringing yourself up-to-date with events in your industry.

Always remember you are the eyes and ears for all your customers and clients as well. Perhaps acting as 'unofficial broker' you can bring two businesses together. Imagine what both parties will think of you then!

The other benefit is that you can use networking for your own personal development, to achieve the goals you have set yourself and ensure you are the success you want to be.

Thought Three

How do you feel?

Sometimes if you think 'happy' your body naturally positions itself appropriately. Conversely, if you put your body in that position first your brain will think: 'I'm in a happy position therefore I must be happy'.

Notice your body posture right now. For example, if you feel sad, your shoulders may be slumped, with your head down, eyes down.

Now smile, have a big grin on your face. Notice your body posture. Your eyes may be looking up; perhaps your head is raised. Shoulders back – you become happier just because you are smiling. Note that position.

Think of a happy moment in your life and capture your body posture. This is how you must be when networking and about to enter a room where you may know nobody. Think happy, know how your body is when you are happy, put yourself in that posture, head up, shoulders back, no tension in arms or legs, feel that posture, relax – and you are ready to make an entrance.

If you can change your mental attitude like that you are truly in command of your feelings.

Thought Four

Take two or three deep breaths. This will naturally relax you. Concentrate on your breathing. Breathe in, hold for 5-10 seconds, breathe out. Do this and relax.

Still not convinced...

Thought Five

You are responsible for your own attitude.

You can bring your own sunshine or your own clouds. You are responsible for your feelings. Do not have a 'victim' mentality where you feel you cannot change circumstances – feel in control of your destiny.

We are able to choose our response to any situation. If we feel defeated, we will be. If we think we are winners, we can be.

I think it was Henry Ford who said, 'whether you think you can or you think you can't, you're right'.

Know what the barriers are to your being successful and be aware of them and their root causes. Name them.

Ask, 'What can I do to remove them?' Challenge yourself. Challenge every justification story you have created to stop yourself moving on. Know that you can succeed.

Viktor Frankl, a survivor of a concentration camp, wrote in his book *Man's Searching for Meaning*:

'The ultimate freedom, the final freedom we have, is the ability to choose our attitude in any given set of circumstances.'

We can achieve genuine 'win-win' situations in networking. Somebody soon will know how you can help them solve a problem. They, in turn, will want to help you.

Thought Six

Neuro-linguistic Programming involves visualisation. Picture success and choose positive words about yourself. Don't verbally beat yourself up. That inner voice, does it say 'you will never be able to do this?' If it does, banish such thoughts and replace them with, 'you can do this, you have so much to offer.'

Remember an event or situation of which you can be proud. How does it feel? Capture that feeling and try to bottle it!

Make a list of all you have to offer. What experiences do you have that will help another person? I have just tried installing broadband and I am sure the lessons learnt would be useful to others thinking of making a similar purchase.

Spend time visualizing success, whether at a meeting or a breakfast seminar or an evening reception. Imagine the sounds, the people chatting, the drink flowing and feel comfortable.

Some of us will be moving out of comfort zones, into areas of stretch in which you can truly develop. Some people only operate where they feel at ease; they know all the routines and can do the job easily. This gives them little room to grow because the challenge is not there. So, moving outside those easy routines into an area that is less predictable can be very worthwhile but it can also be frightening.

Remind yourself that you only grow and truly live when on the margins of what you know you can do.

Thought Seven

There is a great thrill in entering a room and not knowing anyone. The trick is to leave any 'low self-esteem baggage' at the door. Put it into a sturdy case and padlock it mentally. You will then be free to enter the room as a more confident person. You can be whoever you want to be, no one will know.

Thought Eight

Risk/reward ration?

What are the risks?

There are no risks in reality, only rewards. These rewards are the opportunity of meeting interesting people in a convivial atmosphere, keeping up-to-date with business news and – just maybe – the chance to share with someone the benefits of doing business with you and booking an appointment for a further meeting.

What is the worst thing that can happen to you?

How likely is that?

Thought Nine

Think stallion and not mouse

Think 'thoroughbred', be confident, be able to take on all comers. Do not say 'I don't want to be here' and cower in the corner. Feel how good you really are.

Once you have put yourself into the right mental frame of mind, we can look at content.

4. Content Preparation

Thought Ten

Be interesting for 7 seconds and interested for the rest of the time together

You have 7 seconds in which to make an impression, so prepare an introduction that will ensure that someone will want to continue a conversation with you.

If in doubt, remember the chat-up lines you used when you wanted to impress someone!

Focus on not who you are (I'm a banker) but what you do! 'I help people make their dreams come true…' or 'I help businesses achieve the success they desire.'

Some interesting opening lines I have read are:

'… I deal with removals, I remove businesses from where they are to where they want to be.'

'I am a builder… a builder of relationships.'

'I am a revolutionary… I will revolutionise your business.'

Know what is special about you. What distinguishes you from the rest? Everyone is unique and in business you need a unique selling point so this must be introduced early into the conversation.

You should only say enough to make the person you are talking to want to continue the conversation with you.

Then stop and ask about their business. How did they become so successful? What opportunities are there at present for them? What do they want to achieve? What does success mean to them? What challenge do they face? What will make life easier for them?

As time flies by, actively listen and start to ask yourself 'how can I help them achieve that success?' Your thinking or mind-set should be 'What can I do for them?' NOT 'What can this person do for me?'

Having written down your opening seven-second slot ask:

a. Is your introduction engaging? Would someone want to continue chatting to you?
b. Can you say it naturally and make it fit the situation?

Rehearse your opening mentally so it becomes natural to you. Feel you are in the room, hearing sounds, the glasses clinking, people laughing and think about what you are going to say, until it becomes second nature.

I have heard some networkers say their name and spell it out. 'My name is Smith, that's S.M.I.T.H. with an I not a Y.' This can feel clumsy but the repetition does make people remember you.

Thought Eleven

Conversation Starters at Events

You will have your own conversation starters, lines that break the ice but to give you a start, here are a few I have heard:

- *What did you think of the venue/speaker?*
- *What line of business are you in?*
- *How is business?*
- *What is your role in the business?*
- *What did you hope to achieve from this evening, has it met expectations?*
- *What is the market doing, how are you maximizing the opportunities?*
- *Do you network often?*
- *What other interesting venues do you attend?*
- *What was your last holiday like?*

Mention the wine, the food, whether it is in plentiful supply or unusual in any way.

If you worked in a bank you could be blunt and say:

'I am looking for someone who is unhappy with their bank, do you know anyone?' (this might back-fire if they say it is your bank!) but it is a way of trying to talk to people who might provide you with business.

'I'm looking for accountants. Can you introduce me to any?'

When introducing yourself, be sure to give a solid handshake and make good eye contact.

Think of possible common interests, such as sports, holidays, children, school, cars and journeys, news stories, television programmes. Read today's newspaper, read magazines like *The Economist* for up-to-date commentary. The aim is to make connections, to find common ground, anything to create a link and for a deeper conversation to follow. This is all about trust and building rapport.

Have a good answer if they ask you the same question in return, e.g. 'Have you been on holiday yet?' They respond and after saying "and you" what will you say?... Will it be a one-sentence reply, which does not take the conversation forward or will it be a little more:

'I went to Blackpool, I didn't realize how much it had changed from...'

Be ready with up-to-date thoughts on business issues such as regulations, tax, staff, premises, social media – all the subjects that business people routinely tackle and have a story to tell or useful information to pass on.

Thought Twelve

Know what you want to achieve

Ask yourself 'Is this the right event for me? Will I meet the right sort of people here? Is it the right venue in which to be seen?'

Time is important and networking can be hit-and-miss unless you use all these tips, so consider whether this event is for you by double-checking the guest list, speaker and venue.

Thought Thirteen

List five major accomplishments that you are proud of in your life

This will provide you with information about who you are and the types of resources you have available to help others.

If you have achieved something you will have touched many people, created friendships, learned valuable lessons. All of this can be used to help another person who may want to try and achieve something similar.

If you have run a marathon then you have expertise, resources and contacts to share with someone who is yet to run their first marathon.

Ask yourself what are the special skills that you have to offer?

Thought Fourteen

Think of 10 reasons why someone should want to buy from you

You may be thinking of the features of your product or service. Now turn these features into benefits by inserting the phrase... 'which means'... To really drive the point home add a further phrase,'which will result in you having...'

For example, the feature of 18 months free banking means that you do not have to worry about charges which means you have extra money to help your business grow which will result in you having the time to enjoy the reward of your hard-work which means... and so on.

There are many benefits from one feature.

It is the emotions of a person on which you are focusing. Emotions buy!

The heart rules the head.

Thought Fifteen

If you are still thinking, I cannot do this – believe in yourself!

Think about what success will mean to you materially. Will it mean that new car or a holiday or a promotion? This is the desire factor and desire gives energy. Capture and channel that energy for your own benefit.

Thought Sixteen

You ARE the answer to somebody's problem

With networking everyone wins. You will feel good helping solve someone's problems and they will thank you for it.

The mind-set is not 'What can these people do for me?' but "What can I do for these people? If you have problems, I am the solution.'

So find out what the other person's issues are.

- *How can you be of service?*
- *What can you offer?*
- *What do you need?*
- *How can you help?*
- *What can you do for them?*
- *How can you serve them?*

5. At The Event

Thought Seventeen

When entering the room, what do you do?

Look around the room. If a person is on their own, be friendly, say "hello." This is the ideal opportunity for testing your opening sentence. They will hopefully be delighted to have someone with whom to talk.

If you come across a couple talking, leave them alone as they could be deep in conversation and not want to talk to outsiders.

If you encounter a group of three or more, just linger slightly outside the group and you will be asked to join them. It does happen.

If the function started with a talk, find people who asked questions and compliment them on what they said. Speak to the speaker.

Find the organisers, they are there to ensure you have a worthwhile time. They will talk to you and introduce you to others in the room but only if you give them information with which to work. Speak to the person sitting next to you. Speak to people on the guest list who you know or to guests from an industry you know about, so you can show you have in-depth knowledge and find out new information.

Do not look at the guest list and think 'I must find X'. You will spend your time looking at small badges on people's chests and get embarrassed. Better to ask the organisers if they can introduce you to the person for whom you are looking.

Thought Eighteen

When introduced to someone…

To help you remember to whom you are being introduced, try:

- *Hearing the name in your head. Repeat it in your head.*
- *See the person and hold the image.*
- *See the name on a nametag.*

- *Say the name out loud; ask if you have pronounced it properly.*
- *Look at the name when you get the business card.*
- *Review cards at the end of the evening and picture the person.*

Thought Nineteen

Objections

You are there to get business so it is natural to ask 'are you happy with your current suppliers at present?'

They may say 'yes, I have been with them for 25 years'.

You say 'that's good' and think 'bother!'

So why not say:

'Do you drive? Do you have a spare wheel in case something goes wrong? Consider me as that spare wheel!'

'I don't want all your business just a small bit of it and it will keep your current suppliers on the ball.'

The aim is to get a foothold you can use to develop later.

Thought Twenty

Business cards

Have plenty of your business cards available in one pocket and in another, room for putting all the cards you collect. Perhaps have two pockets available, one for cards from guests with whom you have had useful conversations and where you think a business opportunity might arise straight away, and a second pocket for cards that might be useful in the long term, but not at the moment. You never know when a person could be useful to you, your business or even a client of yours.

Write on the back of the card, the date, the event and something interesting you learned about the person.

Have your diary with you so you can arrange a meeting time or arrange a time when you can phone. If your mobile phone has a diary application, ensure it's up to date.

Maintain the initiative. Phone them, do not allow them to ring you, as you want to be prepared for the conversation and ready to book the appointment. If they phone you, it may be inconvenient. Always keep the ball in your court.

Thought Twenty-One

There may be a lull, and sometimes you need a rest from continually talking, so use it to reflect on successes so far. What has worked?

Keep on mentally rehearsing what you are going to say and, as you become more experienced, you can use sentences that you have found to be useful in prompting information from the person to whom you are talking.

Thought Twenty-Two

If, during the course of the event you are attending, you begin to get annoyed for some reason, a tip to calm you down is to say to yourself, 'this is most vexing'.

Use a word that makes the situation more fun. Another example is 'I am particularly peeved at present'. It will make you abandon your current negative thoughts and will prompt you into another, more positive mood.

Thought Twenty-Three

Make a commitment to stay to the end. Otherwise, you will find any opportunity to leave and you could miss out. Sometimes, the best conversations are when majority of people have gone home and you are left with the real networkers.

Ensure that you have a variety of networking opportunities or you could end up meeting the same people at different venues.

Thought Twenty-Four

The ten-metre rule

I heard that when top golfers play a shot they will think about it afterwards for 10 metres, then not think about it again and concentrate on the next shot. Why not try the same principle for your networking? When trying to speak with people, if it doesn't work, there is always another group with whom to speak who are not too far away.

6. After The Event

Thought Twenty-Five

Reflect, after the event

Contact everyone from whom you accepted a card using their preferred method of communication, and see how you can develop the relationship.

Consider, did you achieve your objectives? Was it worth the time and effort? Would you go again? Did you learn anything? What would you do differently and what went well that you would do again?

How are you going to nurture your networking circle? Will you send handwritten postcards saying 'Saw this and thought of you'? Do you have any newsletters you can send? Was there an interesting article in the newspaper that you think might benefit your potential client? You do not want to bombard him or her with notes, just enough to keep you in their mind in a positive way.

Perhaps even send them a copy of this little book!

Is the networking group you have joined diverse enough for what you want?

Know with whom you want to spend time, prioritise them into gold, silver and bronze categories. Then check to see who you think will want to spend time with you. Do they match? If not, what can you do to alter the situation?

It's all about relationships and being professional.

Thought Twenty-Six

Find a role model who is good at networking so that you can copy their behaviour and body language. See how they prepare, the types of questions they ask, the word patterns they use, and so on. It could be an interviewer on television or someone you have seen or know personally.

Thought Twenty-Seven

Can you buddy up with someone?

When embarking on networking, share your experiences with a buddy and tell them how the event went. If it was a disaster, tell the story: it will be fun and the situation will not seem so bad in retrospect. You can then try again. The key is not to dwell on bad experiences, learn from them and move on. Reflect on what went well and what you would change and try again next time. Be encouraging to each other but challenge each other to keep on trying and to improve each time.

Thought Twenty-Eight

Next Time

Be a 'next time' person and not an 'if only' person.

That is, do not say 'if only "X" had

happened' this will make you depressed but think 'next time I will ensure "X" does happen by...'

7. Networking and You

Thought Twenty-Nine

Use your compass

Think of a compass with the points, North, South, East and West. Use this to assess your personal networking circle.

Compass point North: do you need to know more people of a higher standing? How strong are the relationships you currently have with such people?

Ask the same questions about people who depend on you, staff who report to you. This is compass point South.

Look at you personal relationships, friends and colleagues. How strong are those relationships and do you need more of them? This is compass point West.

What is the relationship with sister organisations or partner companies to yours? Does it require strengthening? This is compass point East.

Thought Thirty

Six degrees of separation

I have read that we are within six introductions of meeting anyone in the world. The rationale, I believe, is that we each know 250 people, so if we contact the people they know and they contact the people *they* know and so on, we should reach the contact we want. Surely now with social media a maximum of 250 is easily achievable.

Start with a blank sheet of paper and write 'me' in the centre. Draw spokes out from the centre for family, friends, work, hobbies, church and so on. Draw branches from the spokes of key individuals. Then add connections those key individuals may have and continue spreading out. This is the start of your network.

Whatever the situation you have which needs attention, these people hold the key. They will either know the answer or know somebody who knows the answer.

To use this web you must know what you want to achieve. What is your life purpose? What do you want to achieve this year? Then ask yourself 'Who on this web/network can I contact to help me achieve success?'

As you network, you can add more people to this list. The more names, the more likely it is that they may know someone who can help.

Thought Thirty-One

Odd thoughts

It is etiquette when introducing someone to introduce the junior to the senior, e.g. 'Prime Minister, may I introduce...'

Do ask for business.

Do ask for other contacts. When you are talking to someone, do not be afraid to ask, 'who do you know who might be interested in what I do?'

'Who would you recommend I contact about...?'

Being a director is a lonely job. With whom can they discuss things? You could be an answer to a problem but you will never know unless you ask.

Do a SWOT analysis on yourself. What are your strengths and weaknesses, where are your opportunities and what are the threats you face? Know the many skills you possess. Think what you have to offer. Know that you have much to offer.

Do you look the part? Are you dressed appropriately? If you look good and show you care about yourself, it promotes the professional image you wish to convey.

If you really want to have contacts find a mentor who can help. Find someone who wants you to succeed!

Treat everyone well because they are special, interesting, likeable and fun. Never think otherwise.

8. Speed-Networking Thoughtfully

What is speed-networking?

At a speed-networking event you normally have one minute in which to tell the person sitting opposite you what you do and why they should buy from you.

The person opposite you then has one minute in which to do the same. Then either you or that person moves on and you do the same thing again with another person.

This process can recur up to 20 times or more, so it can be quite repetitive but it perfects your sales pitch beautifully.

Ten Thoughts

For a successful speed-networking event.

1. *Make sure you bring lots of business cards so you have enough for everyone. Give out your card at the beginning, as it gets too hectic at the end of the time. Ensure cards have your up to date contact details. Some times having your picture on the card can help the recipient remember you.*
2. *Know three unique things about your business.*
3. *When you receive someone's card write something about them on the back so you remember them. You can place a card from a potential client who you think will be useful in your right pocket immediately and those who might be useful later in your left pocket so you don't get them mixed up.*
4. *Know what you are going to say that will interest the other person and focus on why you are unique and how you can benefit them.*
5. *Smile so they can feel confident in you.*

6. *Really listen and think not only whether they can help you but also how you can help them and if you know anyone else who might be interested in them.*
7. *The key is to allow the power of reciprocity to work in your favour.*
8. *Follow up with an e-mail of phone call the next day. Don't delay. The next stage is to make an appointment to see a decision-maker. It is vital for you to keep in contact.*
9. *My best tip is this: let them do the talking. You speak for 15 seconds of your minute to say what you do. Then invite them to use the rest of your time plus their minute to tell you what they want to achieve from the speed-networking event. This way you can marry what you offer with what the person in front of you needs.*
10. *Then just remember to ask for the business, it can – and often is – as easy as that!*

9. To Summarise

1. *Know what you want to accomplish on a personal/professional level.*
2. *You only have to be interesting for seven seconds then be interested in your opposite number for the rest of your time together.*
3. *Prepare an introduction that is geared to the event, and internalise it so it sounds natural, not like reading a script.*
4. *Identify several conversational starters appropriate for the occasion.*
5. *Go in with a positive mind and stay to the end.*
6. *Keep the initiative when contacting potential customers.*
7. *Collect business cards using two pockets; you never know when a particular contact will be useful to you or your customers. Note down something interesting about them on the card.*
8. *Gain from every contact you make, try both to get something and to give something to each person.*

9. *Look at their website, understand what the business does and then ring them the day after the event. If you don't ring, send an email, but you must follow up your leads.*
10. *Maintain relationships and help other people to be successful. They will, in turn, recommend you to other people and this will be a far better way of advertising yourself, as personal recommendation will always prove more successful – and it's free!*
11. *The best leaders are the best connected so check how well connected you are.*

Ask for the business. You deserve it.

Lightning Source UK Ltd.
Milton Keynes UK
UKRC02n0749020217
293416UK00018BB/109